IN THE NOISELESS NIGHT

In the

NOISELESS NIGHT

poems about childhood in the 50's

Carolyn Fischer Caines

IN THE NOISELESS NIGHT

Carolyn F. Caines
108 Villa Road
Kelso, WA 98626

ACKNOWLEDGEMENTS
See poem notes at the end of this book
for information about previously published poems.

1st edition

ISBN: 978-1-257-99467-0

In loving memory of my mother
Selma Johnson
who guided me through these childhood days
and whom I miss very much.

Thanks to my poetry group:
to Lorraine, who edited line by line
and made numerous, welcome suggestions,
and to Tammy, Chalet, and Janice,
who encouraged me to keep writing.

Special thanks to my sister
Susan Sloat
who said I should just do this
and wonders why I took so long.

CONTENTS

IN THE NOISELESS NIGHT

Lying on my back,
I draw my feet up close,
making a mountain of the Comforter over me,
fluff of down and Spirit…down
sharing the same name.

Memories flash around me in black-and-white.
My eyes are open,
the room is dark,
but I see pictures in motion,
lives lived,
commotion hushed and all herky-jerky
like a silent picture show.

It is there, in the noiseless night,
that the days, which have fallen 'round
and scattered through the years without leave,
have returned to be excused properly.

MEMORIES THAT CANNOT SLEEP

I'm alone in the darkened room
with all my memories that cannot sleep.
Like orphans they cling to me,
        begging to be held.

I'm not sad,
only weary from their clumsy weight
and their constant, stepping-on-toes dance
        in my head.

I try whispering goodnight,
but they refuse to answer, instead
slip beside me into the cool, white envelope
        of sheets.

In the morning I find them,
those hide-and-seek eyes following me.
All the memories that cannot sleep
        continue to haunt.

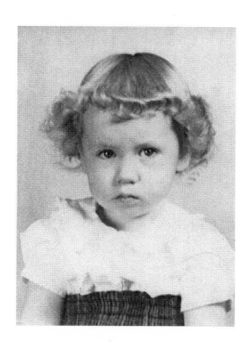

ONLY THE MOON

When I was but a child I thought
The moon was a dish in the sky.
I wondered then, as anyone ought,
Who threw it way up there so high?

When the moon was only half,
I called for my mother to see.
A broken dish! (Why did she laugh?)
She couldn't blame that one on me!

A STORY

October, 1952

Everyone loves a story.
Let's begin with a house.
It sits near a single set of railroad tracks
and the faded arms of crossing posts.
Freight and log cars pass daily,
along with an occasional hobo,
his legs dangling from a boxcar.
Gray shingles wrap around the small house,
its windows trimmed in white.
From the bare cement porch,
a front door opens into a living room.
Dusty maroon, overstuffed furniture
and an out-of-tune piano
rest on a tired, rose-patterned carpet.

In the dining room, knotty-pine paneling
surrounds a large, framed photo,
its convex glass shielding
a shy, blond boy who sits on a stool.

The dining table's chrome legs peek out
from under a starched, white cloth.
Cake plates are ready, placed beside
china cups and saucers, and dessert forks.
The girl will sit on a stool from the kitchen.
Beside her will be one small present
wrapped in white tissue and curling ribbon.

Beyond the dining room, we find the kitchen,
a linoleum floor, and a window over a sink
that looks out to a garden and milk house.
The red-bottomed, metal stool with fold-out step
is ready to be moved to the dining room.
It sits beside a row of white cabinets,
a stove, a humming refrigerator.
The cake with white frosting
sits on the counter beside a knife
waiting for five candles from the drawer.

On the far side of the kitchen, an open door
reveals a bedroom with twin beds,
one with a brown metal frame, one white.
That's where the father reads Bible stories
to the little blond boy and his sister,
the one having a birthday.

Down the hall, another bedroom,
a double bed, mirrored dressing table,
and one tall bureau where
a lace doily cradles framed photos.

A story lives here: a father with a bad heart
from the war, two young children, a country
wife in cotton dress and gingham apron.
Oh, yes, and the plain wooden crib
ready in the corner of the room.

SUDDENLY IN ASTORIA

A hundred years suddenly surround me
as the wind blows in with the sea birds' squall
and the silent cloak of dusk.

I pull the pale hood closer around my ears
against the cool evening, but cannot shake off
bony fingers of time settling on my shoulders.

Along the rusty railroad tracks, I trace a path
of worn footprints beside a rotting pier, its timbers
giving way to the pull of moss-heavy tides.

Here, my own grandmother once stood,
wrapped in a heavy coat against the wind,
watching the tide as her hopes struggled upriver.

We are linked, she and I.
Pacing the shoreline, I feel destiny
step into my shoes beside the wide river.

GRANDMA REETA

I was so young when you left,
but I remember how your straight brown hair
hung loosely from a bun,
how tall four-foot-eleven was to a child,
how your lace-up shoes clunked
on the bare wood floors.

You always wore dresses,
dark prints of stiff material for church,
lighter prints with starched aprons for the kitchen.

Do you know I have your hands, Grandma?
Short, stubby fingers wrinkled at the knuckles,
skin growing more veined and delicate with age.
I want to feel your hands again.

I see you in my mirror some days.
High forehead, firm brow,
green-gray-brown, mixed-up calico eyes,
sturdy nose and thin lips,
determination set in a rounded chin.

I wish we could talk.

THE LANGUAGE IN MY BONES

My grandparents grew up in the north woods,
farming village of Puolanka, Finland.
In the early 1900's, war threatened to steal their sons,
social class dictates shadowed their future,
and unrest marched like a giant on the horizon.

Willing to leave their homes forever, these pilgrims
carried their stubborn determination intact
across the ocean to America, becoming a community
of transplanted Finnish culture.

Grandma spoke no English, and Grandpa
spoke enough to get along when he went to town.
My mother learned English in a one-room school.
Sometimes a hard schoolmaster punished children
for slipping back into their native tongue.
These second generation children thought little
of their bilingual life, school and home.

The third generation didn't learn Finnish.
I remember only a few words Grandma spoke
when she called my brother a bad boy!

I recall the sound of it, the hum,
the swelling syllables of conversation
over cardamom bread and coffee.
My brother and I nibbled squeaky cheese,
trying to be invisible while the thin, white cheese
squeaked wonderfully between our teeth.

Years later, European Finnish relations
who dared the long trip to visit us,
marveled at the difference in the language.
Their Finnish had changed with the times,

while Finns here had awakened, much like
Rip Van Winkle, to find their native night
had actually lasted over forty years.

Awakening in a new day with an old language
didn't bother Grandma much.
American Finnish was just fine with her.
Mother laughed about it because she used it rarely,
like an old pair of slippers.

And I? Sometimes I wonder what I missed,
not knowing Finnish. Or is the language
in my bones somehow, along with the bread
and coffee and squeaky cheese?

CHRISTMAS EVE 1952

Columbia Heights Finnish Congregational Church

At midnight, headlight beams bounce
across the grass. A stream of black autos
rumble into the field, parking in uneven rows
near the country church. Engines silence.
Fathers and grandfathers open heavy, car doors.

A girl in black Mary Janes jumps out
onto a running board, followed by a grandmother,
her hair held neatly in a bun. Moments later,
the girl's mother emerges, taking her hand.

They join other families walking in the shadows
toward the church steps.
Men in dark wool suits and hats greet each other
in rumbling Finn, with firm handshakes.
Foggy breath hangs in the air
while the women urge them inside.

Wooden pews are dwarfed by a fir tree.
Arched boughs nearly touch the high-beamed ceiling.
Candles glow on branches like earthbound stars.

Sliding across a hard pew, the girl hums *Silent Night*.
Finnish lyrics fill the sanctuary
as the pump organ wheezes out the final chords.

The pastor reads the Christmas story in Finnish,
then English: *Today in the town of David*
a Savior has been born to you; he is Christ the Lord.

Drowsy, the girl leans into her mother's coat sleeve,
the melody of another carol, like a lullaby in her ears.
All is still a moment, and then a rush of cold air when
the church doors open behind them.

Wide awake now, the girl strains to see Santa
with his bag. Her mother whispers to her,
and she steps out timidly from the pew
with the crowd of eager children
waiting for a midnight Christmas sweet.

MANDOLIN MUSIC

It disappeared one day. No one knows when.
My small hands had memorized the feel of
its highly-polished bowlback, it's slender neck
and frets. When nimble fingers plucked the strings,
music floated out in a plink-plinking rhapsody.

I like to imagine Grandma dancing a little jig
in her Sunday, lace-up shoes, the swish of
her skirt, and my own small hands clapping,
keeping time with a haunting mandolin refrain.

Grandpa sips dark coffee at the kitchen table,
toe-taps slapping the faded, linoleum floor.
He hands me a cup of coffee-laced milk,
and we dunk our cardamom bread together.

THE
FAMILY TREE
has
all these branches
scattered here and there,
outlined in
documents, deeds, certificates,
postcards, and
letters written in Finnish
with flowing, fading, ink pen script.
I can't comprehend how
Grandma and Grandpa's family
birthed so many cousins and children of cousins
I've never met.
Perhaps when we were small,
our mothers shared coffee and pulla bread
while we sat listening to them talk.
When I meet you,
I see how we
are so
alike,
a family
with long
roots   that hold
us   all   together.

CHEEK TO CHEEK

I remember her rose-scented skin,
soft and smooth,
when Mom held me cheek to cheek.
No matter how my day had gone
or how I might protest,
she simply pulled me
into the circle of her arms,
quite near her beating heart.
I felt at home there, a part of her.
If I could feel her cheek to cheek
once again, I'd hold on a little longer.

When I close my eyes to pray,
sometimes I hold my face up
waiting for that kind of feeling,
waiting with a sigh.
I imagine how the Father watches,
how He may smile, softly
bending cheek to cheek with me,
His child.

POETS ANONYMOUS

I was four: *The Tall Book of Mother Goose*
tempted me. Little Miss Muffet sat,
curds and whey dripping down her chin
while Spider slid down beside her.
It was spine-tingling.
I asked for it again and again.

I learned to do the hand-clap, knee-slap version
of Pease Porridge Hot, taking perverse pleasure
thinking of children eating mush made from peas.

By the time I was eight, I was addicted.
Not knowing this, my mother enabled me.
She presented me with a copy of
Sung Under the Silver Umbrella,
a fitting title because I hid my addiction
under the covers at night, flashlight in hand.
I couldn't quit saying:
>   *Mary Middling had a pig,*
>   *Not very little and not very big.*

The honeyed words flowed smoothly,
intoxicating music to my young soul.
I dreamed of sailing away with the owl
and the pussycat in their pea-green boat.
Or with Wynken, Blynken, and Nod
in their wooden shoe.

I thought the five little monkeys deserved
what they got for teasing Uncle Crocodile.
I imagined that *my* mother would give *me*
animal crackers and cocoa for supper.

A child no longer hides
under the blanket of night.
My name is Carolyn.
I am a poet.

GOOD TIMES

patterned after Lucille Clifton's poem

My daddy sat on the cast iron bed
reading from the faded-blue, Bible storybook.
He was Moses, and we were the children.
So-o-o many children
so long ago.
Pajamas and stories,
and they were good times,
good times,
good times.

My mother stood behind me
while I squirmed on the red, kitchen chair.
Fingers and damp hair whirling in rhythm,
pin curls tied up in a scarf,
I'd be beautiful tomorrow.
And they were good times,
good times,
good times.

Child, you grow up, but always remember
the good times.

GONE TO FETCH A RABBIT SKIN

Bye, Baby Bunting,
Daddy's gone a-hunting,
To fetch a little rabbit skin
To wrap the Baby Bunting in.
--English rhyme,1784

The rabbit hutch door cried out
on rusty hinges, closing us in
against the sound of geese
running free and the scent of
iris and gladiola near the gate.

Daddy held the rabbit by its hind legs,
its soft, lifeless body dangling
and swaying like the pendulum
of our kitchen clock. In slow motion
I saw the slice of knife

and the pull, one great tug turning
what was inside, out,
relieving Rabbit of her coat of fur,
pink flesh hanging naked
before my wide-eyed stare.

The lines of "Bye, Baby Bunting"
hummed through my head.
I thought of soft rabbit skin
in some baby's cradle
and rabbit stew.

IN THE RABBIT HUTCH

In the rabbit hutch she sits
Upon her web-wire floor.
Now she crouches, now she sniffs,
Now scratches at the door.

A bit of sunshine filters in
Between the slats of wood.
She twitches up her nose at it
And thinks how life is good.

A carrot, lettuce, rabbit food
Appear inside her dish.
She always has enough to drink,
So what more could she wish?

Little Rabbit turns around
And backs out of the cage.
She stretches to her full height.
It's time you act your age!

Too bad a little girl is told
Look, you are such a mess!
She was only playing when
Poor Rabbit tore her dress!

COWBOY BEDSPREADS

I found one in an old cardboard box
the day we began cleaning out Dad's garage.
Lifting up a corner of the faded bedspread
brought back the faint smell of childhood.

When we were young, my brother Franklin and I
had no walls between us. We shared a bedroom
in our small, gray-shingled house near railroad tracks
where freight trains rattled by in the night.

His brown iron bed frame sat against one wall
and my white bed against the opposite one.
We had matching brown and cream bedspreads
with little cowboys riding horses inside fences.

They threw lassos overhead, stitched in a brown sky,
like our dreams that floated side by side
in the dark, no distance at all between them.
We are grown now and lasso wild mustang words,

pulling them back into our own brown sky,
not letting them escape across the fences.
My brother and I see the world with weathered
cowboy faces as we ride our tired horses home.

CATLIN HALL

Floors swept, garbage taken out,
the dance music put to bed,
late Saturday night
the transformation has begun.

Guitars and fiddles packed away,
a pulpit takes center stage, piano nearby,
hymnals stacked and ready.
Folding chairs that had circled the room
face front in neatly-spaced rows.

Dance hall turned church overnight,
redemption complete.
Families enter Sunday morning
in their best clothes and shined shoes.

Children sit for Sunday school lessons
taught on flannel boards,
where felt men are marched
across a flannel wilderness
with their felt wives and camels.

Students memorize Bible verses,
reciting them for a small reward,
a star on a chart,
a picture card stapled to a ribbon.

*   *   *

At the age of five, I was a serious child
who entertained serious thoughts,
like God and heaven and hell.
Call it a spiritual inclination
or simply a heart for God;
whatever the reason, I believed early.

I remember praying earnestly
about small things,
like my missing hairbrush.
The moment I finished praying
and opened my eyes, I saw it
on the bottom shelf of a rolling cart
in the kitchen. Amen and amen.

The day my brother, Franklin, prayed
with Mother to become a Christian,
I said I wanted to do that too.
I could see the question in her eyes.
Was I too young? She prayed anyway.

We knelt together by our sofa.
I buried my face in my arms,
my nose in the dusty maroon cushion,
and I asked Jesus into my heart.
How simple the act; how profound it felt.

The following Sunday night, my father
took me to church where I stood to testify.
The congregation smiled, nodding
approval, and I took my first communion.

Faith was natural, salvation certain,
at Catlin Hall that night.

AT BLACK LAKE

The white canvas tents lined up again,
stretched out at their corners by ropes
tied to pegs driven in the dirt.
Short wooden walls and rough floor boards
served as a permanent base for each tent.

Stepping inside our assigned tent,
I noticed where last night's rain had dripped
through the canvas leaving wet spots
on the half-walls and floor planks.

Rolling out my sleeping bag on an old army cot,
I lay down listening to the flap of stiff canvas
in the afternoon breeze
and studied the black specks on the tent walls.
Musty odors lingered where the sun
hadn't yet bleached them out,
and my sleeping bag smelled of sawdust
and plaid-flannel memories.

I came here every summer with my family
for a week of tenting and camp meetings
in the old, timbered sanctuary
with its hard wooden benches and sawdust floors.
Singing from a well-used hymnal, I watched
the pump organ grind out its nasal notes
while the out-of-tune piano pounded out
the enthusiastic chords of *Onward Christian Soldiers*
and the majestic notes of *How Great Thou Art*.

Year after year, preachers and missionaries
stood behind that rustic pulpit
painting vivid word pictures of the Lord's return.
I shivered in awe, knowing we could be scooped up
at any moment, to fly away through the night.

After the sermons, altar calls quickly filled
the front of the tabernacle. Seeking God,
earnest souls knelt in the sawdust.
A kid would have been pretty callous
not to have settled up with God
right then and there.

The final night of summer camp
often found us gathered around a campfire
near the lake's edge, where dark waves
slapped against the pebbled shore.
My heart pounding, I took my turn with others,
both young and old, testifying of my new resolve
to serve God. Then in a symbolic gesture,
I, too, tossed my small piece of wood
into the flames and watched how the sparks
skittered into the dark across Black Lake.

EASTER BASKETS

In the far corner of the attic, I found them,
the Easter baskets from last year.
Thoughts of dyed eggs and an Easter
from my own childhood crowded in as I sat
pulling at stray scraps of dusty green "grass."

Back then our baskets were small props
for table decoration or a family photo.
Beside a potted Easter lily, my brother and I
had posed for the camera. Franklin wore
suspenders with his tweed pants, a bowtie,
and his white Sunday shirt. A slick wave
had been combed into his blond locks.
A budding smirk gathered on his lips.

The camera caught me with eyes half shut
and a bashful smile. Feeling like a princess
in my Easter dress, I sat in a small folding chair,
ankles crossed politely, patent leather shoes,
not yet scuffed. My hands are cupped carefully
around the small Easter basket, holding it
the way you would hold a fragile memory.

IN INDIA CHILDREN

In India children are starving
Mother's tongue plied guilt at suppertime
Pushing peas around the plate
I wondered what the postage would be.

Mother's tongue plied guilt at suppertime
Shame to waste a bite
I wondered what the postage would be
How far away was India?

Shame to waste a bite
Feeling full of peas and guilt
How far away was India?
America's children are very full

Feeling full of peas and guilt
Standing an ocean apart
America's children are very full
Could have been a beggar's child.

Standing an ocean apart
Holding a fork over my supper plate
Could have been a beggar's child
And grateful for the mission handout.

Holding a fork over my supper plate
In India children are starving
And grateful for the mission handout
Pushing peas into their mouths.

ELVA

Her name had a mysterious flavor
as it rolled off my tongue. Taller than I,
she wore her hair in long, blond ringlets
that flew out behind her, goddess-like, as she ran.

One fall, our mothers accidentally bought us
the same dresses from Sears Roebuck.
Fascinated, we studied each other,
mirror images in grey-and-red plaid.

Like her reflection, I followed Elva everywhere.
She lived across the railroad bridge
in a camp of small, silver trailers
parked beneath a grove of oak trees.

She led the way. I listened as her brown oxfords
scuffed from one tie to the next
across the bridge. I never looked down,
just kept humming softly to myself.

Once I stayed the night. Elva and I shared a bed
with her little sister, who slept at our feet.
In the dark, lights from the neighboring drive-in movie
flickered on the ceiling, a strange sort of night light.

Branches swished across the metal roof,
drumming a haunting counterpoint
to Elva's steady breathing. I lay still,
holding my breath 'til morning.

LIGHT UNDER THE DOOR

Lying in my solitary bed,
its white wrought-iron frame, my halo,
I pulled the scratchy wool blanket
firmly under my chin.

Still as the mouse that had eaten
her way into my bedroom wall,
more still even than that,
my eyes focused on the thin trail of
light under the door.

Spidery, beams crawled across
the dull, wood floor.
Dusty puffs of words blew under,
disturbing the evening quiet.

Rising and falling, the words crept
up my back and into one ear.
I wished I could not hear them and
pulled the blanket over my head.

But having to know is braver
than not knowing.
I peeked and listened and hoped...
caught in the trance of the light
under the door.

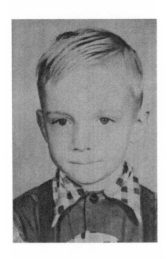

WHAT HE DIDN'T KNOW

The whole day was quite ordinary.
He woke expecting nothing else.
Some of it was plain boring, to tell the truth.
Fried eggs and toast,
jeans with the knees worn thin,
an old plaid shirt,
thick-soled sneakers with frayed shoelaces,
Dad calling him outside to help
clean the rabbit hutches.
A July day like any other.

It should have been a wonderful surprise,
the birthday party that night,
but he stood quietly, tears filling his eyes.
It had been his birthday all day
and he hadn't known.

WHEN I WAS YOUNG

Psalm 37:25 I was young, and now I am old.

I wanted to be older.
      Now I am, but wish I weren't.
I wanted to be taller.
      Now I am, but not much.
I wanted to stay up all night.
      Now I can, but I'm too tired.
I wanted to have a room of my own.
      Now I can, but I'd rather share it.
I wanted to eat anything I liked, whenever.
      Now I can, but I dare not.
I wanted to be done with school.
      Now I am, but I want to learn more.
I wanted time to go faster.
      Now it does.

When I was young, I had no clue.

BEHIND THE HOUSE ON FERRY STREET

Sweet pea and gladiola breath
scent the summer afternoon
as I lie in the grass face up,
eyelids fluttering, now open, now shut.

I hear rabbits shuffling in wire cages,
and picture small, furry noses
twitching nervously while furry thighs
push against squeaky, pen doors.

Nearby, geese pad across packed dirt
on webbed feet. In the midday heat,
they make rude comments
to small bugs who don't listen.

A gentle puff of air crosses my forehead,
tickling like goose down, a wakening wand
so light, so slight, I barely feel it. And then
the sky opens, blue against dark eyelash fringe.

My toes curl involuntarily, gripping blades of grass
that make my bed. Through sleepy eyes,
I focus on a small bee, its face buried
inside a dandelion. Suddenly it flies in a tight circle,

darting directly past my nose and over the fence
where the geese are watching me now, no idea
what it would be like to awaken anywhere else
than here, behind the house on Ferry Street.

THE ROAD IN FRONT OF OUR HOUSE

The road in front of our house
lay like a wide open yawn,
its shiny black tongue
fascinated me when I was a child.

It began with the gravelly-bending,
upward incline of the driveway
between our gray-shingled house
and the old dairy, milk-house.

Lying nearby on my stomach
in the freshly cut grass,
I could peek out, eye-level with the road,
observing the passing black autos

spitting dust in my face.
The road south led to the intersection
where mailboxes sat cattywampus
on shaky wooden posts

and where paper mill smokestacks
broke up the skyline,
their sulfurous smoky breath
often drifting our way.

Here, too, was Ben Pullen's Service Station,
tempting me with penny candy
and nickel soda bottles that clanked crankily
out of a big, red, vending machine.

A round man in oil-stained overalls,
Ben greeted us with a friendly smirk
and a tip of his faded beanie.
I'd walked there with Dad just to chat.

The road north sometimes chilled me.
Not far down the asphalt, orange-peel top
lay a railroad track with steel rails
right along the boundary of our property

marked by foreboding, black-lettered
RAILROAD CROSSING X's. The shrill whistle
of a far-off engine startled us several times daily,
followed by rattling freight cars shaking the ground.

Across the tracks, the nighttime glow
of the drive-in screen whispered secrets
muffled by silent, soldier maples.
Sometimes Dad would park our car

by the side of the road so we could
watch the forbidden figures playing
across the white screen. There, they took
giant steps, dancing in the night.

The road in front of our house led me,
wide-eyed, into the world.

MOUSEHOLE

I stared at the mousehole gnawed through
the baseboard behind my bedroom door.
Shadows played across it at bedtime,
and I knew a story lived inside that wall,
a story somehow connected to the late-night
struggle in the kitchen behind the fridge.
Dad regularly set mousetraps baited
with bits of yellow cheese.
The snap and scuttle in the dark
told me he'd been foiled again.
I could almost see little mousy grins
as they raced away with a cheek-fat prize.

I recall a favorite children's book about Ralph,
a mouse who lived behind a baseboard
in an old country inn. From his mousehole
in a guestroom, he ventured out
to ride a small boy's toy motorcycle.
Such fearsome pleasures of hiding and
discovery were in the pages of that book,
and more recently, a video I shared
with my grandson, Jack.

Jack was seeing more than I, the day we checked in
for a stay at an old Victorian, three-story B&B.
After inspecting the lobby and wooden staircase,
we found our way down the polished hallway
to our room, complete with antique furnishings:
an iron bedstead, oak bureau, and mirrored wardrobe.
Jack pulled me close, whispering in my ear,
"Where is it?" This he asked in awe, all the while
casting furtive glances about the room.
I'm thinking, *What?*
"The mousehole!"

IN A GARDEN GREENING

In a garden greening just beyond the back door,
I remember squatting down to watch pea pods.
They dangled from their curling vines
amid a web of string strung like a cat's cradle
between thin-fingered poles.

At my side stood a plumping cherry tree
where rows of silver pie tins hung
like Christmas ornaments clinking in the hot sun.
Startled sparrows fled, but not the fruit-pecking
        blackbird.

I remember the awe of popping open one fat pod
and finding peas inside. I hated peas,
the limp, off-green kind you might find floating
languidly in the murky waters of a tin can,
but these baby-green orbs tempted me.

Sliding a thumb along the slippery pea pod belly,
I rolled the tiny peas into my palm,
examining them momentarily before selecting one
and lifting it cautiously to my lips. It crunched
between my teeth, flesh bursting.

Surprising sweetness slipped down my throat.
Like a garden greening, I unfolded
my own spindly legs, a pod flying in the wind,
and a handful of summer rolling about in my palm.

IN-AND-OUT

It was a new-fangled thing,
the terra cotta building with its
aqua, paddle-shaped roof sticking out
over a freshly paved drive-through.

You drive up to the sliding window,
order a few burgers, pay a dollar,
pocket the change. You hear meat frying
just beyond the screened window.

We had to try it once at least.
In-and-out we drove,
with our greasy burger trophy tempting us
the whole three-blocks home.

That it tasted better than Mama's might be
because of the yellow wrapper and
mystery sauce. Or perhaps simple novelty
salted our tongues. Daddy said it was

pure waste to spend so much when
Mama did it better at home. She smiled.
Take one last sniff of the yellow paper.
We wouldn't be going In-and-Out again.

TEST PATTERN

The day our television arrived on Ferry Street
was a colorful day. The mysterious box
with its fuzzy screen squealed in the corner
of our living room. Outside on the roof,
Dad could be heard pounding and hollering
down to my mother as he set up the antenna.

Sometime before dark, the picture appeared
in focus with its black-and-white people
moving about on the little screen. Jackie Gleason
and The Honeymooners brought us all into
a small apartment where *Alice!* was hollered
into our memory forever. It was the first show
and all too soon, it ended.

On the screen, the National Anthem played,
flag flying, and then the test pattern appeared.
No more television until tomorrow afternoon.
An Indian's face in profile surrounded by designs
let you know the television was working.

I don't know how many minutes we stared
at that ridiculous, little Indian. He remains
a part of my childhood along with Mr. Moon,
Howdy Doody, and the Mickey Mouse Club.
My brother gravitated to Zorro or The Lone Ranger.
We played cowboys and Indians, and he liked
to be the Cisco Kid. *Hey, Pancho!* Was that me?
Only two or three channels, but so much to see.

The television antenna had to be aimed
in the right direction for each channel.
Dad rigged up a handle by the window,
and with a few cranks, the roof-antenna rotated.
Nothing could be done about the test pattern though.
We'd live with that mute Indian a few more years.

CHRISTMAS SECRET

Secret sounds of Christmastime
Could drive a child nuts ...
The wrapping paper rustling,
A bedroom door that shuts.

One day I heard the muffled creak
Of Mother's dresser drawer,
A click of padded hinges,
And the bench legs scrape the floor.

Running to the living room,
I grabbed my paper dolls.
Pretending to be occupied,
I had not heard her calls.

Later when I had the chance,
I crept into her room.
There I found the box, a ring.
Yes, it would be mine soon!

A childish deceitfulness,
My secret promptly spilt.
How had Mother known my crime?
I couldn't hide my guilt.

While I cried, confessed my sin,
She wiped away my tears.
She promised she would never tell
Our secret through the years.

Still every time I wear that ring,
Those pink stones set in gold,
I think of love, forgiveness, too,
How Mother never told.

EVENING IN PARIS

If I could swim into glass,
slipping down
through cobalt waves
of Evening in Paris,
I might be able
to bottle time
or stop it altogether.

The scent clings
faintly
in an empty bottle,
to a chipped silver top,
to the lining of my memory.

A bottled evening,
Paris parted without a farewell,
no singularly sweet memory,
only the scent
that slowly
fades.

THE VITAMIN EATER

By the time my father unscrewed the lid
of the Watkins vitamin bottle,
my stomach had already knotted in panic.

I could not swallow the burgundy capsule,
no matter the pep talk, threats, or oceans of milk.

Soggy and limp, it stuck to the back of my tongue
until I spit it out on the dinner plate.

And then came the knife. The abused capsule
was sliced in two and squeezed until
its brown, mustardy insides lay across
a torn chunk of bread like a burnt sacrifice.
It smelled the same.

However many times the scene played,
it always ended the same.

                    *   *   *

This morning I swallowed a handful
in one gulp.

WHEN I AM IN THE KITCHEN

The past stares at me from a shelf,
beckons to me from an open drawer.

The Bo Peep pitcher in a cream-colored skirt
looks down from her glass shelf, reminding me
she'd spent many cold winters behind a row
of canning jars in the garage before I rescued her.

Beside her sits a handled, brown bowl
my mother used for extra pumpkin pie filling.
I can almost smell the spicy aroma when I hold it.

A single, white bloom pokes from the neck
of a small, ceramic bud vase.
Painted black with white and red drips
down the sides, it is simply inscribed with
gold lettering, *To Mother "58"*. I was ten.

An assortment of china cups and saucers
line one shelf, patiently waiting for teatime.
It hasn't been done right since Mom's cousins
sat around the table eating a sampling
of cookies and cakes while I poured tea.

In the bottom drawer, the recipe box overflows
with clippings and hand-written notecards,
but I can't find the one I want, my mother's
pork spareribs recipe. The typewriter print
has faded and the card is spotted with sauce.

When I am in the kitchen, the past whispers,
and I pause to listen.

THE LAST PICTURE

Last pictures are not typically the best,
often with mouth open to the world.
No time for proper good-byes,
cold, dark-eyed stare. I saw him like that,
lying in the milk house, his ear to the floor,
but not hearing the sound of pills
and pill bottle spilling and scattering.

I don't want the last picture, please.
Can't you take it back and fix it properly?
Comb his hair and sit him upright
in a chair, my hand on his shoulder perhaps.
Color him alive. I need to see him that way.

Or make the last picture be of him
fastening the tiny, gold locket around
my neck. I have the locket still. I can
hold it, warm in my hand. I can remember
the feel of his fingers on my neck.
Make that be the last picture for me.

BOXING

A box
small, white, satin-lined
a ring inside
two pink stones set in gold
given to me at six
Snap the lid shut on Christmas past.

A box
glistening in the rain
The box is long, white, satin-lined
my daddy inside.
I am eight.
Snap the lid tight on childhood past.

DADDY'S GONE

A little girl of only eight,
a sadness now to contemplate.
The grownups float in circled talk,
their whispered words as pale as chalk.

Daddy, I need to hear your voice.

Alone, I'm left with feelings raw.
It can't be true. What is the flaw?
Did robbers in some evil plot
take my Daddy? Had you thought?

Daddy, is that you stepping on the porch?

I stare forlornly at the phone.
Someone will call now that we're home.
They'll say it was a great mistake.
I'll hear you call and I'll awake.

Daddy, I need you to come back!

I can't remember things I should.
You're fading now where once you stood.
How tall were you? Your hands, what size?
What was the color of your eyes?

Daddy, I need to see you again.

Do you hear the prayers I've said?
And could you tuck me into bed?
Could your hand just touch my face?
Do you see me in this place?

Daddy, I need you to hold me.

We have to move now that you're gone,
hold up our chins and carry on.
I'll make a picture in my head--
our house, this room, my white-framed bed.

Daddy, will you know where I've gone?

Being brave and standing tall
don't seem to help-- the tears still fall
in silent pools way deep inside
where I am drowning in their tide.

Daddy, are you crying, too?

WHY I DISLIKE CARNATIONS

Walking past the fresh-cut flowers
on my way to the dairy case,
I am reminded how much I dislike
the scent of carnations,

a persistent innuendo from the past.
I remember carnations
in bouquets and gaudy wreaths
with stiff, white ribbons.

They outlast roses, they do.
But why would anyone care?
One day is long enough.
Who will come to see them tomorrow?

They are not welcome to follow me home
and sit brightly on the kitchen counter.
I do not wish to smell them again, ever.
Too many carnations and tears mixing

with the smell of earth and grass beneath my feet.
It's enough they should hug the casket,
don't ask me to take them home,
these carnations, the scent of grief.

FUNERAL FOR A BIRD

Cousin Tom stood in the empty lot
reverently peering over the top of his Bible
at the spot where a small hole had been dug
and the creature ceremoniously laid out for burial.
The cause of death, I do not know, but we,
the mourners, stood still observing, too,
the lifeless form.

Cousin Ruth clasped her hands together,
lifted her eyes toward the blue sky,
opened her mouth wide, and sang
the solemn notes of a funeral song.
Something about heaven and hope and such.

Cousin Dan, who dug the small grave,
patted the dirt back gently over the stiff form
of the dearly departed-- bird.
Standing sentinel with the shovel handle clasped
to his side, he saluted. *Job well done, bird.*

I remember this funeral for a bird
in the same summer I lost my father.
I remember it the same--
Sermon. Sad song. Kleenex goodbye.

SUMMER OF '56

We lived with my aunt and uncle
that summer, twelve in the house.

I shared a bed with my cousin Ruth.
I was eight; she, a teenager.
She knew the lyrics of pop songs,
had her own radio set in her room.
We played Easy Money and Parcheesi.
I kicked in my sleep. She kicked me out
despite my pretending to be asleep
and lying so still. Moved into a room
with my mother, little sister,
and baby brother.

A neighbor girl rode stick horses with me,
brooms actually. Her mother fixed us
peanut butter and jelly sandwiches.
I ate, hoping to acquire a taste for them.
Vicky said her dog could speak.
Amazing! I thought.
She tossed him a scrap. *Woof!*
Didn't think that was speaking.

We all went along when Uncle Leonard
preached in a country church.
Aunt Ines played the piano, and Ruth
often sang solos…with shoes on.
She liked to slip them off during church.
Her brothers snagged them one night
and slid them back several rows.
She sang in stocking feet quite well.
Later Ruth chased her brothers
round the graveyard by the church.
Uncle frowned a lot on the way home.

That fall Mother rented a house of our own,
across town. Just five in the house.

MARILYN AND CAROLYN

Our names rolled against the tongue in rhyme,
which made us smile when we first met.
Marilyn lived a few doors down, we were
nearly the same age, and she was Catholic.

The proof lay on the coffee table
in her living room: a Catholic Bible.
It looked like ours, but inside were names
of books I'd never heard in my Bible.

Marilyn looked normal, except for
the plaid skirt and white blouse
she wore to school. Private school.
When she changed into pedal pushers
and a sleeveless blouse, she looked like me.

Marilyn and Carolyn. We wiled away Saturdays
roller skating. After fastening the skate clamps
to our heavy-soled oxfords with a key,
we'd zip down the rippled sidewalks
watching for cracks in the pavement.

And when we tired of that, there were
Barbie-dramas played out in my backyard.
Marilyn had Ken, who always acted wicked,
but Barbie liked him.

It was in the backyard, we became
perfume makers, connoisseurs of scent.
Crush a handful of rose petals with rocks,
stir in water, and bottle it. Ah!
Scents sometimes more stinky than not.

Marilyn and Carolyn. Our names rhymed.
How strange is that?

THE SODA FOUNTAIN

Red, upholstered, chrome stools,
ten in a row-- we chose the middle two,
my friend and I, spinning side-to-side
to see if they worked properly.

Our saddle shoes and ankle socks
swayed impatiently while the lady
behind the counter pulled a pencil
from her hairdo and tapped the counter.
What'll it be, girls?

Marilyn held out a dime for a Coke
With two straws, please!
Eyebrows raised (Did she think we were rich?)
the waitress tossed two straws our way,
at the same time, setting a glass under
the fizzy stream. Fountain Coke. No bottles.

Her back to us, we both (partners in crime)
tore the paper off one end of our straws
and blew upwards, watching the straw papers
fly up to rest behind the Soda Fountain sign.
Ah! We sat smiling into our shared Coke.
The thrill of it made us giddy.

TELL YOU A SECRET

I'll tell you a secret.
As a child I listened once
to such a confidence.
I told a secret, too, a soul secret.

She had lied. She'd made up hers!
Laughing, she told my secret,
didn't care
that it felt like someone peeling my heart
and putting it in a display window.

Disbelief and betrayal
sat sour in my stomach.
I've forgotten her name
but I remember her disdain.
A curtain of innocence fell away.

Don't tell secrets
to just anyone.

WOOLWORTH'S FIVE-AND-DIME

On a Saturday afternoon, I hopped on
my green Schwinn 3-speed and rode up
15th Avenue to the lake.
May sun soaked me in optimism.

On a mission, I navigated the east end
of Lake Sacajawea, ignoring the temptation
to look for ducks. Instead, I crossed over
toward Commerce Avenue until I spotted
Woolworth's, its red sign beckoning,

I leaned my bike against the building,
pushed open the glass door, and stared.
At ten I was tall enough to see over
endless counters of buttons, combs, barrettes,
curios, and more. I'd know when I found it.

I'd wandered half the store, when a waitress
behind the lunch counter stopped serving
and smiled at me. I smiled back, wishing
I could sit awhile on a spinning stool. Instead,
I searched down another aisle.

And then, there it was. Perfect.
A huge, framed picture of flowers in a white vase.
I didn't know the flowers' names, I just knew
the blue and purple blossoms with some white,
pink, and yellow were exactly right
for my Mother's Day gift. The money in my pocket
was enough; the saleslady beamed
as she wrapped it in brown paper and twine.

Somehow I managed the ride home
with the huge parcel balanced across the bike's
handlebars and my fist grasping the twine.

I think Mother loved it as much as I did.
Though it cost only a few dollars,
she never replaced the print.
For the rest of her life, it hung on the wall
by the fireplace in her living room.

Today I noticed the picture has warped,
as time will do with most of us, but I'd never
give it away. It hangs by my fireplace,
a piece of childhood I can touch.

PAPER BAG LUNCHES

Monday mornings meant
sack lunches like this:
two slices of white bread
lie bare-faced on the counter,

awaiting a slathering
of mustard and mayonnaise,
thinly slice onion
and yesterday's roast beef,

sandwiches wrapped
in wax paper
and placed in plain brown
paper bags, no frills.

> * * *

Sent to clean my bedroom,
     one I shared with my brother,
I'm certain it was his lunch bag
stashed in the back corner of the closet.

A squashed paper bag,
     an old sandwich inside,
with great disdain, I held it at arm's length
and promptly marched into the living room

where Mother was entertaining
     a gentleman visitor. I didn't know
my mother could get so upset, like
I'd revealed some horrible, family secret.

Who was this man, anyway?

SHAKE ON IT

My mother's dress hangs in the attic
next to my own wedding dress.
Neither one will be worn again,
but some things can't be given away.

Lacy pink material, modest V-neck,
three-quarter length sleeves,
and a knife-pleated skirt.
She wore it the day we got a new dad.

The gentleman caller was a Swede,
We called him Mr. Johnson. A bachelor
come recently from Minnesota,
he had this notion about our mother.

An old photo revealed the truth.
It was ground-breaking Sunday
for the new church. At the ceremony,
my mother is looking right at him,

not eyes front, like everyone else.
He was brave to even show up
on our doorstep, with four children,
all wondering why he visited so often.

Wasn't long, and we knew. Ceremony,
sermon, kiss. We ate cake and shook hands
in the reception line like everyone else.
Welcome to our new dad.

ORGAN MUSIC AND
A SPARKLER-TOPPED SUNDAE

Eating out with a family of seven didn't happen often.
This was a special occasion, my twelfth birthday.

Dressed in our Sunday best, we followed the hostess
past the cash register, past Mrs. Nolte at the organ,
to the back of the restaurant and a large booth.
I slid across the slippery upholstered seat,
while everyone else shuffled for positions.

Holding the menu, I felt older already.
What we ordered was forgettable;
I was waiting for dessert.
It couldn't come soon enough.

I knew the routine, yet my heart beat faster
when the organ music paused. A chord sounded,
and the strains of *Happy Birthday* filled the restaurant.
Everyone sang along and turned to see the waitress
carrying a magnificent ice cream sundae
with a sparkler on top, right to our table.
She set the sundae in front of me, sparks flying.

When the song concluded, everyone clapped.
The sparkler fizzled out with one last flash.
I knew what was expected of a polite young lady,
so I made my way timidly to the front of the
restaurant, curious eyes following me.
Mrs. Nolte had begun another selection,
her feet dancing on the pedals, her hands floating
over the keys. She smiled at me and nodded
when I said thank you.

I don't remember any presents that birthday,
but I'll never forget the organ music
and a sparkler-topped sundae.

BIRTH OF A POET

Mr. Altman's eighth grade history class,
not the typical classroom.
Desks sat in a huge square, no outsiders,
front-row teacher's pets, or back-row sliders.
Everyone in view.

We discovered debate; we argued
both sides of history. Why have slaves?
Why not? Get the facts. Think before you speak.
Be creative. Take a chance.

Who would dare write a poem about a battle?
About the fall of Quebec? How would you
describe the look of the Frenchmen
surprised in battle? Peach pies?

The French did blink and blink their eyes,
Till they were as big as peach pies.

Immortal, those lines, making their way
in broad daylight, my first published poem
in the school paper, *The Husky Howl.*
Can't you hear the howling?

Those were the true birth pains
and baby babble of a newborn poet.

WHO LOVED A BOOK

At twelve she was shy and awkward.
She had just moved to a new neighborhood,
acquired a new dad, and started middle school.
Changes unsettled her world.

Then she found it, shoved back on a dusty shelf
by the north windows in the school library.
A faded green cover with gold imprint:
Johnny Appleseed.

Hidden away in her room,
the words began to march off the page,
creating a character she must have admired,
though now she can't recall many details.

She wanted to keep the book forever
and postponed its inevitable surrender
to the stern-spectacled librarian
who wouldn't understand how the book

had captured her blossoming spirit.
She would have "lost" that book
and happily paid the fine, but for her
conscience that wouldn't warrant a lie.

A lifetime later, I recall that girl
who loved a book.

IRONING

I can see her in a simple cotton dress,
hair in pin curls wrapped in a scarf,
knotted on top of her head.
She irons on a creaky, padded board
with a laundry basket nearby.

I'd watched her earlier,
wielding a glass pop bottle,
its shaker top attached
for sprinkling water.
She properly baptized the shirts
and rolled them up like great sausages
before putting them in a plastic bag.

She taught me how to iron:
pulling a rolled-up shirt from the bag,
she shakes it out
and begins with the collar,
pressing first the top side
and then underneath.

Sleeve fronts, then backs,
shoulders all around,
shirt front, side, back,
other side, and front again.
I can hear the sizzle and steam swirling
with each press and swoop of the iron.
There was an order in her love.

RABBIT TRAILS

The grass was flattened
    like pancakes in a stack
        weighed down with syrup
            leaving little puddles
        and sticky fingers,
    so you have to wash again.

The grass was flattened
by furry, bunny feet
    not like the kind,
        hard and stiff,
            dangling from a chain
        in your brother's pocket
    next to the house key.

The grass was flattened
by furry, bunny feet
that escaped
    like a midnight train
        across the river,
            whistle blowing
        in the dark,
    sending shivers up your back.

The grass was flattened
by furry, bunny feet
that escaped
the rabbit trap
    cold confined space
        under an apple box
            with a stick tied
        to a string that you pull
    while you are hiding.

The grass was flattened
by furry, bunny feet
that escaped
the rabbit trap
in the yard.
>   where my brother
>   had target practice
>   with his BB gun,
>   and where the BB
>   ricocheted near his eye.

The grass was flattened.

ROAD TRIPS

Count the miles between here and there,
Between Washington and Wisconsin,
between Ohio and Minnesota.
Count the rivers and bridges,
the roads winding through mountains,
the long miles of plains and farmland,
the motel rooms where maids are cleaning,
changing sheets, dusting, dusting.

A family tumbles into the car as the father
checks off a mental list: milkman, paperboy,
mailman. Yes. Striped cardboard suitcases
and sack lunches are stashed in the trunk,
while children elbow each other in the backseat.
Pillows on the floorboard. Pillows propped
against a door. The sky is still dark this morning,
and the children doze off to the rumble
of the tires on the road. Father knows the drill.

Don't take their mother on a road too near a cliff.
She would nearly faint, breathing hard and refusing
to open her eyes until it was safe again.
Don't drive too fast. Don't pass unless you can see
a mile ahead. Be prepared to stop by three
in the afternoon. Mother has to inspect the motel
room before a child can step one foot inside.
No, you can't use the bathroom before she decides.

The father's German relations, in Milwaukee,
the Fischer men, raise bottles of dark beer in the yard,
while women made strudel and gossip
in the cool basement rooms, and cousins race
through the field. Uncles snap pictures of families,
photos that will fade in an album or a shoebox.

In Ohio, an uncle's farm. The older children
shoot BB guns at paper targets and catch fireflies

in the dark. Uncle didn't have much schooling,
but he knows about respect. Use Thee and Thou
when you pray. God speaks King James English.
Uncle freely lectures the older children. *Don't call
your baby brother a stinker,* even if he is one.

The mumps come visiting in Ohio, too, a white, linen
towel wrapped under the girl's chin and tied
on top of her head. Does it hold in her puffy cheeks?
Prevent them from falling to her chest?
Great time to be relegated to the sofa in the parlor.

On a road trip, the father makes roadside stops
when no gas stations are in sight. The children
run around, releasing cooped-up energy.
Father shakes baby brother upside down,
by his heels. Get the sand out of his pockets
before letting him back in the car.

Halfway across Nebraska, they pull up
under the awning of a drive-in hamburger joint.
First thing, the father asks about restrooms.
A distracted, bubblegum-chewing waitress
drawls, "Sorry, we only have Dixie-cups."
In the backseat, sisters snicker,
while younger brother grimaces in pain.

In Minnesota and Wisconsin they visit Swedish
relations. Like the old woman who lived in a shoe,
the uncles and aunts have children everywhere.
Cousins and more cousins, even a liturgy of girls
with names that all begin with J: Janelle, Janyce
Jeannie, Julie...

And always, it's the food that brings them together.
Potlucks, picnics, casseroles, and Jello salads
that jiggle on a child's plate. Aunts and uncles
sip coffee, and tell stories of times long ago,
down other roads.

SMELT RUN

Every year in December or January,
the seagulls gathered, greedy birds flying low,
swooping down the Cowlitz River.
Didn't take long for word to get out.

Cars and trucks lined Westside Highway
from Kelso to Lexington. Women and children
carried buckets and stood waiting on the riverbank
as men wielded long-poled nets in the current.

People claimed the smelt jumped right out of the river
into their buckets. Sometimes their nets strained,
and one dip would fill a pail. Only six inches long,
those slippery, silver fish caused quite a commotion.

They were a treat for us. Mother gutted a mess
in the kitchen sink, cut off their heads,
dipped them in flour, and fried them to a crispy,
golden brown. That was dinner.

My brother and I made a contest of eating them.
We'd both set a paper towel by our plates,
gently coax open the belly of a smelt, and pull its tail,
removing the backbone in one, feathery piece.

Each backbone was lined up side by side
on the paper towel, memorial to our hunger.
Mother kept frying, and we kept eating.
Who was the winner? The tally would tell.

Even today, when I hear the smelt are running,
I'm counting fish spines in my head.

HAMILTON 3-4585

Picking up the heavy, black handset,
the dark cord tethers me to the base
with its rotating wheel and finger holes.
Dialing is an art form:
finger in correct, numbered hole,
rotate wheel clockwise to the stop bar,
lift finger out and wait for the whir
as the wheel resumes position.
Seven times and you're done.

The Seattle World's Fair
showcased the newest technology,
including a pushbutton phone.
Fascinated, my brother Franklin
(a year older than I, and too confident)
challenged me to a race.
He'd do the pushbutton phone,
and I'd get the rotary dial. Okay.

With lightning speed I poked
my dialing finger into the holes
for HAMILTON 3-4585 and sent
the wheel flying round and round.
The familiar trumps the unfamiliar.

It did this time at least.
I was grinning before Frank finished
pushing the last number.
A big overhead screen announced
the victory of the rotary phone.
So much for progress.
I wonder who would answer
If I dialed that number now.

THE RESPONSIBILITY OF A NEW HATCHET

--for my brother, Vernie

Dew still dotted the rhododendron blooms.
Bees slumbered in their hives.
The boy, young enough to skip,
carried what could have been a toy
but for the glint of the single blade.

In the maple grove a bird pecked the ground,
fiercely pulling a fat worm from the earth.
Overhead came the cry of hungry babies.
One hand to his brow, the boy paused,
scanning the trees briefly
before trudging on through the woods.

Reaching the crest of a hillside,
the boy circled a sapling that grew upward
from the slope, trunk bent to the sky. It would do.
He gripped the hatchet with both hands,
and after making one light tap against the tree
to mark his target, he pulled back and swung.

The sapling shook to the topmost limbs,
a small quiver, hardly noticeable.
Again and again the hatchet moved in an arc,
landing against the side of the resilient, little maple.

All day long, the soft thump, thump
of the boy's hatchet echoed over the wood.
He could have quit when the first painful blisters
rose in protest on his tender palms.
But each time he stopped, it was only
to examine the fine line made by the hatchet
cleaving the maple.

A SUNDAY DRIVE

Sunday dinner dishes had barely been cleared away,
when Dad backed our yellow Plymouth out of
the garage, and the whole family climbed in for a ride.
Didn't matter where, perhaps a place with a creek,
stones for skipping, and a meadow of flowers.

Flowers were important this time because
I had a wildflower collection to finish for biology.
My nose to the window, I scanned
the roadside for bits of color.

There! Dad pulled the car to the side of the road.
I pushed the heavy door open, leaving it hanging
over a ditch, while I ran to pluck
a wildflower from the roadside bank.

The Plymouth, with its tail fins and wide bench seats,
was not small, and the county roads were not wide.
Dad watched nervously for other Sunday drivers.
The car idled, and my brothers yelled for me to hurry.

My little sister held the specimens in a paper bag.
Sometimes Mother insisted there was no place
to pull over. I could only look out the window
and sigh about the wildflowers left behind.

AT THE KIDS' TABLE AGAIN

We sat, crowded around the chrome-legged,
kitchen table with faux wood, Formica top
and vinyl upholstered chairs.
No linens here, just Mom's everyday dishes,
an assortment of glasses scratched and hazy,
and paper napkins neatly folded by each place,
with a fork and spoon, no knives for kids.

Vernie squirmed nearby in his maple high chair,
impatiently slapping his hands
on the cracked wood tray.
Stevie perched himself on the metal, kitchen chair
with fold-down step. Susie sat on a catalog
so her chin was nearly parallel to and hanging over
her red castle dinner plate.
Being the oldest kid present, Franklin claimed
the chair at the head of the table
while I played hostess at the other end.
Our cousins sat on folding chairs
brought in from the garage.

Grown-up conversation drifted in from the dining room
where the white linen tablecloth muffled the sounds
of forks and knives and serving dishes being passed.
Ice cubes clinked in crystal water goblets.

At the kids' table, dumb jokes and laughter prevailed
with almost always some spilled milk.
Green beans often stood upright, soldiers
in gravy-laden potato hills, while olives proved to be
valued finger ornaments. Never enough chicken
drumsticks to go around; the last ones served
had to settle for bony chicken backs
or scrawny chicken wings.

DIVIDING MEMORIES

Standing in the house I'd known
Since I was only ten,
Sifting through my memories,
I pause, I sigh, and then,

You choose a teacup set for you,
And I pick one, bright pink.
We linger long that afternoon
Sweet memories we drink.

A Bible marked and worn with use,
A squeaky rocking chair,
Some glasses lying on the desk,
A brush with strands of hair.

I pick a memory for me,
And you pick one for you.
Dividing memories is hard
But what's a soul to do?

We'll take our pick of treasures home,
And stories we will tell.
We'll talk about the years gone by,
Dividing memories well.

MY HOME NO MORE

The old red paint and striped awning gone,
new double-pane windows
and roof shingles.
I drove by in search of proof
I'd lived there.

A recent addition jutted out into the yard
where my bedroom wall had been.
Childhood woods had been carved out
to hold a large workshop,
trilliums trampled, ferns torn up.

Three young trees sat side by side,
where our cherry tree had been.
No tart cherry pies.

I looked for the Ponderosa Pine.
I'd planted it as a seedling fifty years ago.
It was gone, the huge tree
reduced to a bump in the lawn.

I wondered what had changed inside.
Did they pull off the wallpaper,
install a dishwasher,
remove the water heater from the kitchen?

My childhood lay beyond the new front door,
the locks changed.

THINKING SEASON

Standing alone at the window,
I scratch against frosty memories of laughter.
Days with pudding-thick delight settle in my stomach
and pumpkin spiced arms reach around me.

A slow minute pauses between coming and going.
I move to close the door
while time settles in the room, nut-ripe,
not hard-shelled and scarred by the fall.

I'm growing wonder from thin air
without soil or water that you can see.
I'm thankful for the late blooms
brought safely indoors before winter.

RESIZING THE DAYS

Yesterdays pile up
like snapshots in random order
flashing across the mind.

Click on a scene with too much sky
and crop the why right out of it.
No need for so much grass,

assumptions beneath your feet. Crop
the thing until emotions lie exposed,
nose to nose with facts in focus.

If the day comes up short, choose
the space it should fill and magnify
the memory in the frame.

If the day was oversized,
too much to bear, make it small
and smaller still.

Poem notes: inspiration for and publishing credits

At Black Lake: Church camp near Olympia, WA.

At the Kids' Table Again: inspired by a reunion of Sunday School friends at my Aunt Lolly's house, when we ("girls" in our 50's and 60's) were at a table separate from our elders.

Behind the House on Ferry Street: began at a workshop with Tim McNulty, Lower Columbia College, 2008.

Birth of a Poet: a writing prompt from the Washington Poets Association, 2011.

Boxing: at a workshop with Joseph Green from LCC, during the Skagit River Poetry Festival, La Conner, WA, 2004.

Catlin Hall: The Evangelical Free Church rented the building in Kelso.

Cheek to Cheek: inspired when attending Time Out--For Women Only Conference, Seattle, 1998, with singer Kathy Troccoli.

Childhood Home: the house on Ferry Street, reading *Poemcrazy* by Susan Wooldridge.

Christmas Eve, 1952: workshop with John Daniels, Lower Columbia College, Longview, WA, 2010.

Christmas Secret: December of 1953

Cowboy Bedspreads: in the room Frank and I shared on Ferry Street.

Daddy's Gone: written during counseling many years later.

Dividing Memories: the days we sorted through the house on Columbia Heights.

Easter Baskets: when we lived on Ferry Street until the summer of '56.

Elva: friend who lived in The Oaks Trailer Park.

Evening in Paris: my mother's perfume. The poem was published in *The Salal Review*, Lower Columbia College literary magazine; spring, 2006.

Family Tree, The: published in the *Cowlitz Historical Quarterly*, Dec. 2010, for a recently-discovered cousin, Maila Cadd.

Funeral for a Bird: when we lived with Uncle Leonard and Aunt Ines.

Gone to Fetch a Rabbit Skin: after reading "Mink Farming" by Murray Anderson.

Good Times: thoughts of Mom and Dad, Selma and Steve Fischer, after reading Lucille Clifton's "Good Times."

Grandma Reeta: for Elsa Reeta (Wayrynen) Juntunen and from inspiration after reading *Poemcrazy* by Susan Wooldridge.

Hamilton 3-4585: after reading *Saint Ben* by John Fischer.

In a Garden Greening: Sergei Duniec's garden. He was a friend of my father during WWII, a fellow German-speaking American.

In-and-Out: the first drive-in burger joint I can remember, on California Way.

In India Children: a pantoum, written because my mother said this to make us clean our plates.

In the Noiseless Night: after reading Thomas Moore's "Oft in the Stilly Night."

Ironing: inspired by David Young's poem, "Mother's Day".

Language in my Bones, The: about my mother's Finnish family, the Juntunen's and Wayrynen's.

Last Picture, The: the untimely death of my father at the age of 36.

Light Under the Door: published in *The Salal Review*, 2004.

Mandolin Music: for Reeta and Thomas Juntunen.

Marilyn and Carolyn: on 15th Avenue in Longview, 1957.

Memories That Cannot Sleep: after reading "Spleen" by Ernest
    Dowson.

Mousehole, The: the house on Ferry Street, *The Mouse and the
    Motorcyle* by Beverly Cleary, and my grandson Jack's
    inspection of our B&B in LaConner, WA.

My Home No More: on Columbia Heights.

Only the Moon: My mother told me I must have seen too many broken
    dishes after tossing them from my highchair. Read at the
    Moon Viewing at the Japanese Garden in the Washington Park
    Arboretum, Seattle, WA, Sept. 2, 2006. Published on the
    Washington Poets Association website.

Organ Music and a Sparkler-Topped Sundae: The Longview
    Restaurant on Commerce Avenue; Mrs. Nolte, organist

Poets Anonymous: inspired by poet Kathleen Flenniken, LaConner,
    WA, at the Skagit River Poetry Festival, 2008.

Rabbit Trails: on Columbia Heights; a writing prompt from my poetry
    group

Resizing the Days: cropping old photos

Responsibility of a New Hatchet, The: my youngest brother, Vernie,
    when we lived on Columbia Heights.

Road in Front of Our House, The: Ferry Street, Longview.
    Honorable Mention in *ByLine* Magazine New Talent Poetry
    Contest, 2004.

Road Trips: a compilation of many years of travel with family.

Smelt Run: Kelso, WA, Smelt Capital of the World

Soda Fountain, The: at the St. Helen's Inn on Oregon Way in
    Longview. Honorable Mention in *ByLine* Magazine's Free
    Verse Poem Contest, 2005; Special Mention in *Writers' Journal*
    Poetry Contest, July, 2006.

Story, A: written after reading "A Story" by Philip Levine.

Suddenly in Astoria: a reflection while walking a pier in Astoria where
    my grandmother once lived after immigrating from Finland.

Sunday Drive: after reading "So This Is Nebraska" by Ted Kooser, U.S.
    Poet Laureate, 2004-2006.

Tell You a Secret: betrayal by a childhood "friend." It was inspired
    when reading *Poemcrazy* by Susan Wooldridge.

Thinking Season: Honorable Mention, *ByLine* Magazine Autumn
    Poem Contest, 2004.

Vitamin Eater, The: after reading "The Potato Eaters" by Leonard
    Nathan. My dad was a part-time Watkins salesman.

What He Didn't Know: my brother Franklin, age seven or so.

When I am in the Kitchen: inspired by a poem of the same title by
    Jeanne Marie Beaumont.

Who Loved a Book: while attending Kelso Junior High.

Why I Dislike Carnations: my father, grandfather, and grandmother,
    all dying within a few years of each other; Honorable Mention
    in *ByLine* Magazine'sStormy/Blue Poem Contest, 2004;
    published in *The Salal Review*, 2006.

ABOUT THE AUTHOR:

Carolyn Caines is a third-generation resident of Southwest Washington State. She and her husband Michael have three children and seven grandchildren.

During her college years, she began writing and published a dozen short stories. A graduate of Seattle Pacific College, she taught grades K-4 and high school English for thirty years.

Carolyn wrote a novel about her Finnish grandparents coming to America, and an article about them, "Sisu Defined Grandparents' Generation," appeared in the *Cowlitz Historical Quarterly.*

She has been writing mostly poetry for the last fifteen years, having published more than 125 poems in *devozine, Evangel, The Salal Review,* and various other magazines, journals, books, and newsletters. Since 1998, she continues to write *Poems For You*, a weekly e-mailing.

You may send a message to her at:
carolyn.caines@facebook.com.

CPSIA information can be obtained at www.ICGtesting.com
Printed in the USA
BVOW040854200911

271684BV00001B/17/P